BIG CAT CONSERVATION

CONSER

PEGGY THOMAS

BIG CAT
CONSERVATION

The Science of Saving Animals

TWENTY-FIRST CENTURY BOOKS
BROOKFIELD, CONNECTICUT

FOR DANNY

Acknowledgements
I'd like to thank the wildlife scientists who shared their work with me, especially Bonnie Yates and Ken Goddard at the National Fish and Wildlife Forensics Laboratory, Chris Keiber and David Brigham at the Buffalo Zoological Gardens, Tom Logan of the Florida Game and Freshwater Fish Commission, Sam Wasser of the Center of Wildlife Conservation, and Kathy Quigley at the Hornocker Wildlife Institute.

Cover photograph courtesy of Animals Animals/Earth Scenes © 1987 Lynn Stone
Photographs courtesy of The National Audubon Society Collection/Photo Researchers: pp. 2 (© Aaron Ferster), 6 (© Alan & Sandy Carey), 22 (© Aaron Ferster), 23 (© Jeff Lepore), 45 (© Ron Austing); Animals Animals/Earth Scenes: pp. 9 (© Anup Shah), 13 (© Lynn Stone), 34 (© Peter Weimann); R. Chris Belden: pp. 14, 15; Mark A. Lotz/Florida Game and Fresh Water Fish Commission: pp. 17, 57, 58; NGS Image Collection: pp. 19 (Michael Nichols), 53 (Chris Johns); © 1999 Seattle Times: p. 21; © Craig Packer: p. 26; Hornocker Wildlife Institute: p. 28 (© Howard Quigley); © Alan Rabinowitz: pp. 30, 31; © 1999 Zoological Society of San Diego: pp. 36, 37 (both); © Gerry Ellis/ENP Images: pp. 38, 41; © Vance Martin/The WILD Foundation: p. 43; U. S. Fish and Wildlife Service: pp. 48, 50 (both)

Library of Congress Cataloging-in-Publication Data
Thomas, Peggy.
Big cat conservation / by Peggy Thomas.
p. cm. — (The Science of saving animals)
Includes bibliographical references (p.   ) and index.
Summary: Examines how scientists and zoos around the world are managing wild and captive big cats like panthers, cheetahs, tigers, and lions by radio tracking, scat examination, zoo breeding programs, and habitat conservation.
ISBN 0-7613-3231-6 (lib. bdg.)
1. Felidae Juvenile literature. 2. Wildlife conservation Juvenile literature. [1. Felidae. 2. Wildlife conservation. 3. Cats.]
I. Title. II. Series: Thomas, Peggy. Science of saving animals.
QL737.C23T4736 2000
333.95'97516—dc2l   99-37434 CIP

Published by Twenty-First Century Books
A Division of The Millbrook Press, Inc.
2 Old New Milford Road
Brookfield, Connecticut 06804
millbrookpress.com

CONTENTS

A Siberian tiger, largest of the big cat species, lopes across a snowfield.

1 WHY SAVE THE BIG CATS?

Looking at Boris, a Siberian tiger, in his zoo enclosure, I can't imagine how heart-pounding it would be to meet him in the wild without the 30-foot (9-meter) moat or thick pane of glass between us. Boris puts his paws up on the glass and I measure my hand. If he were to stand he would tower over me by several feet. He's beautiful, and I'm glad I can come to the Buffalo Zoological Garden any day to see him.

Like most of the Siberian tigers in the world, Boris was born in a zoo. There are far fewer Siberian tigers in the wild. They are disappearing fast, along with Asian lions, snow leopards, the Florida panther, the jaguar of South America, and other big cats.

Wild cats, like many house cats, are independent and secretive. They don't want anything to do with humans. Yet people are fascinated by their beautiful coats, piercing eyes, and sleek bodies. And partly because of our fascination with these exotic creatures, the big cats of the world are in trouble.

BIG AND LITTLE

There are 37 different wild species in the cat family (*Felidae*), ranging in size from a 3-pound (1.4-kilogram) black-footed cat to the 700-pound (318-kilogram) tiger. Although all felines are not the same, they all have a few similar characteristics—a short round skull with powerful jaws, scissorlike back teeth, and sharp pointed canines. All cats purr, but only cats with the Latin name *Panthera* (lion, tiger, leopard, and jaguar) can truly roar. While 30 of the cat species are small, weighing less than 45 pounds (20 kilograms), only seven are considered the big cats. Many cat species include a number of geographically separate populations, or subspecies. While tigers represent only one of the seven big cats, there are five living subspecies of tiger.

Virtually all cats are endangered or threatened in some part of their habitat. They have been killed to protect livestock, and hunted for their fur, meat, and bones. They have been made into trophies, clothes, and medicines, and kept as pets. The hunt still continues, but today the biggest threat is shrinking habitat. Land that used to be wild is being made into farmland and communities. Saving wild cats is a difficult task. It's expensive, time consuming, and sometimes dangerous. So why save big cats?

Tiger (*Panthera tigris*)

There are five types, or subspecies, of tiger left in the world, the Bengal, Indochinese, Chinese, Siberian (or Amur), and Sumatran tigers. The Caspian, Javan, and Bali tigers have become extinct in the last 50 years. Once widespread and abundant over southern and eastern Asia, tigers have been pushed into smaller and isolated pockets of habitat in Russia, China, India, and other countries in Southeast Asia. Researchers estimate that there are anywhere from 4,000 to 7,000 tigers left in the wild. The largest cat in the world is the Siberian tiger, tipping the scales at 700 pounds (318 kilograms). Tigers are solitary animals, preying mainly on large deer. They can eat up to 75 pounds (34 kilograms) of meat in one sitting.

The impressive teeth of a Bengal tiger in Rajasthan, India

BIG CAT CONNECTIONS

Besides being big and beautiful, cats are an important part of their ecosystems, connected to all other living things by how they live and behave. Cats, as carnivores, meat eaters, are at the top of the food chain. The decline of a carnivore changes the balance among other animals and plants in its habitat. Cats prey on smaller carnivores and plant eaters (herbivores). Herbivores compete with one another and affect the plant community. A change in the number of big carnivores in a habitat eventually affects every creature down to the smallest species. The absence of a cat species may cause problems that scientists don't even know about yet.

Cats are also sensitive to changes in the environment. A decline in their population alerts scientists to other problems occurring in the area. The same changes that affect the cat may in time affect the people of the habitat as well.

But in one way, cats are lucky. They are cute, cuddly-looking, and fun to watch, and more people care about their survival than they do about the future of smaller, less attractive animals. Zoo officials have even reported that people spend more time observing cats and other large mammals than they do reptiles, for example. And people will save what they care about.

TEAM WORK

Cat conservation is a team effort. Not just one scientist, or one field of study can solve a problem that has taken hundreds of years to create. To be successful we need to stop poachers, preserve the habitat, learn about cat behavior and how they survive in the wild, and take care of the individuals we have in captivity.

Most of the scientists who work with big cats are biologists. They study living things. But not all biologists look at the same problem in the same way. Some work on a large scale, tracking animals over thousands of acres, and mapping large tracts of land, while others work through a microscope aimed at the inside of a living cell. Scientists from all over the world, and from all types of sciences, are working on their piece of the conservation puzzle. Researchers in a lab help law enforcement stop tiger poaching, while field biologists in Florida learn the secrets of the rare Florida panther. Zoo scientists study cheetah behavior, breed snow leopards, and continue to develop new ways to ensure that cats have a future in the wild.

2 HIGH-TECH TRACKING

Before scientists can protect an animal species, they have to find it. Twenty years ago the Florida Game and Fresh Water Fish Commission set up the Panther Project to count and track one of the rarest big cats in the world—the Florida panther, a subspecies of the American cougar. Only 30 to 50 adults are left in the wild.

Studying an animal in its natural habitat is usually done by field biologists who collect information and study how an animal lives in the wild. They learn what an animal eats, how it breeds, and how much land it needs to survive. But panthers are secretive animals and not many people, even biologists, have seen one. So the information has to be collected by watching for signs and following the animal's movements from the air. Collecting detailed information lets scientists better understand exactly how nature provides for cats, and how we can ensure their survival.

Florida Panther *(Felis concolor coryi)*

The Florida panther is a subspecies of the still numerous cougar that lives in the western United States. Separated by distance from other cougars, the Florida panther developed its own physical traits—becoming smaller, with longer legs and smaller feet than its western cousin. A true Florida panther weighs up to 160 pounds (73 kilograms), and can be identified by the upward turn at the end of its tail and a cowlick, or swirl of hair, on its back. Its fur is reddish brown on the back, with tan sides and a pale gray underbelly. Like most big cats, panthers live solitary lives. Today they survive mainly in southern Florida's national reserves and surrounding private land.

SCAT AND SCRAPES

Sometimes biologists have to think like a cat. They learn what a cat's resting spot looks like, where a female's den may be hidden, and the signs of an animal's last meal. Paw prints called pugmarks show where a cat has walked, in which direction it was headed, how fast it was moving, or even how many kittens a female had with her. The size of the paw print gives the researcher an idea how large the panther was, and whether it was male or female.

Like other big cats, panthers have large territories they defend. Because they can't be everywhere at once, they mark their territories with their scent. They scrape together mounds of dirt and leaves piled over droppings, called scat, or urine. Wildlife biologists eventually learn how to identify an individual from its scrape marks, and can analyze the scat for hair and other remains to learn about the cat's health and what it ate. Larger cats like the tiger also leave their scent on trees, scratching the bark like a house cat at a scratching post.

But scat and scrapes don't tell biologists the whole story or answer questions such as how far cats roam, or how they raise their young. Studies in zoos provide data on reproduction and

The Florida panther, an elusive animal, is smaller than the cougar.

other behavior that is difficult to study in nature. And high-tech tracking equipment allows biologists to follow the elusive cats from a distance. But before they can track one of these big cats they have to catch one—a difficult process that can take days.

UP A TREE

Before sunrise a team of four or five biologists and several dogs set out in swamp buggies. As they near areas where a panther is known to live the biologists then strike out on foot, carrying all the heavy

equipment and safety gear on their backs. Wildlife biologists borrowed a technique that hunters have used for more than a century—sending dogs out to chase down the cat. Dog handler and expert tracker Roy McBride leads the pack, letting the hounds run free. At the first whiff the dogs are off, racing to catch up with their prey and chase it up a tree.

A treed panther is not easy to get down, and the scene is noisy as the dogs yip and paw at the tree trunk until they are pulled back to let the scientists do their work.

The first job is setting up an inflatable cushion to prevent the cat from falling and injuring itself. Part of the team spreads out a huge, round nylon cloth fitted with seven large pockets. The other team members whirl in circles to fill plastic trash bags with air, or blow them up like balloons. When about 30 of these bags have been tied with twine, they are stuffed into the pockets to create a crash bag to place beneath the panther in the tree.

From down below a veterinarian judges the health and weight of the cat and decides on the proper dose of tranquilizer the cat will

It's just a question of time till the tranquilized panther falls onto the crash bag.

need to put it asleep just long enough for the team to get their work done. The drug is measured, loaded into a dart gun, and fired into the cat's hind leg.

Everyone waits until the panther eases into sleep. If it's resting safely on a branch, one of the team members will have to climb up, tie a rope around the cat, and slowly lower it down into the net waiting below.

COLLARED

After the cat is checked by a vet, it is fitted with a radio collar that measures about 2 inches (5 centimeters) wide and weighs 1½ pounds (0.7 kilograms). Each collared cat receives a number, and its transmitter is programmed to give off a unique signal that can be tracked on land for 1½ miles (2.4 kilometers). This isn't much range when the typical male panther has a range of 300 square miles (777 square kilometers). Because the brush is so thick in panther country, biologists track by airplane. From the air the signal can be detected from 15 miles (24 kilometers) away.

The panther project team keeps track of about 36 collared panthers roaming 2 million acres (810,000 hectares) of land. Three times a week a pilot and biologist fly several thousand feet above the ground until they hear a signal. The pilot flies in that direction and spirals down to about 500 feet (153 meters) so they can identify the type of vegetation the cat is in. The location of the signal is marked on topographic maps and logged on a computer. Over several months the biologist will plot more locations on the map, and like connect-the-dot drawings, will build an accurate picture of the panther's movements, how it interacts with its environment, and with other panthers. Twenty years worth of data has taught scientists a lot about the Florida panther and will be used in future planning of parklands and community developments.

BIOLOGIST-IN-A-BOX

Tracking a female panther not only provides information about her life, but also about her kittens. Panther Project coordinator, Darrell Land, admitted that he gets suspicious when a radio-collared female stays in the same place for several days. She might have given birth to a new litter. Field scientists go out to the site when the female is away and set up a "cellular telephone" so they can periodically listen in. They call it a biologist-in-a-box because a biologist used to have to stay by the den 24 hours a day to monitor the family's activities.

Inside the weatherproof box, a cellular phone is hooked up to a receiver. It is positioned 100 to 200 yards (91 to 183 meters) away and can only pick up the signal of the female's collar when she is close by the den. The audio portion of the receiver is connected into the telephone. The researchers can dial up the receiver from any location and get the transmission from the collar. "If the female is near the site, we pick up the collar and hear the beeping tone,"

This panther kitten will lose its spots as it grows older.

said Tom Logan, endangered species coordinator for the commission. "If she's away from the den we don't hear a tone at all, and we use that opportunity to go into the den site to handle the kittens for the first time."

UNDER THE SKIN

Each panther kitten is implanted with a transponder under the skin. It's really just a high-tech identification tag that looks like a tiny metal microchip, and it is coded for each individual panther. It is inserted with a large surgical needle just under the skin on the back of the kitten's neck. The code can only be "read" by a handheld receiver passed over the cat. For example, Logan explained, "The team tries to collar the kittens when they are about seven to eight months old. But if we can't and we have an opportunity to capture one later on, and we suspect that a cat might be from a particular litter, we can check by calling up the transponder."

Sending a Signal

The transmitter is a high-tech mini radio station that only plays one tune, a "beep-beep," sent out on the airwaves at a unique frequency. The only ones who can hear the tune are the researchers with their receiver set at the same frequency. The transmitter is housed in a brass canister about the size of a pocket pager. Airtight and surrounded by shock absorbers, the transmitter is built to survive the bouncing and jostling a panther can give it. The antenna extends out of the transmitter into the collar fabric. To keep the parts together they are sealed in a waterproof epoxy.

The signal from the collar is picked up by either a handheld antenna that looks like the letter H lying flat on a metal rod, or the antenna can be attached to the wing struts of a small airplane.

The transmitters do more than signal the location of a cat. It can tell if the cat is on the move. The signal beeps 60 beats per minute when the panther is at rest, but increases to 70 beats per minute when the panther's head is in motion. Another switch activates a very fast pulse rate if the transmitter is motionless for more than 2 hours. It's a sound biologists dread hearing because it usually means the cat is dead.

CANDID CAMERA

While biologist Ullas Karanth was tracking radio-collared tigers in Nagarahole National Park, India, he kept finding tracks of unknown and uncollared cats. Capturing a tiger to fit it with a radio collar can take months and be very expensive, so Karanth used another piece of equipment to capture the tigers on film.

Karanth set up a series of 15 photo stations. Each station is located in a specific spot that corresponds to a grid on a map. He sets up two cameras, one on either side of the trail. "Individual tigers and leopards have unique coat patterns," he said. "But you need to have matched photos of both sides of the animal."

Dense vegetation in such a large park makes it almost impossible to get a total count of all the animals, so scientists have to estimate by taking a sampling of the area. Karanth doesn't get photos

Biologist Ullas Karanth's remote cameras in Nagarahole National Park, India, made this collection of snapshots.

of every tiger in the park, but with the help of a computer model he can find out what percentage of the population he has photographed, and then estimate the total population.

The best part of using cameras is that they are noninvasive, which means they don't disturb the tiger. "You don't have to catch and handle the animal," Karanth said.

But working in the wilds of India can be dangerous even for a camera. One tiger took a serious dislike to Karanth's expensive camera equipment, bit the camera, pulled it off the stand, and carried it away. Passing elephants have been known to rip the cameras apart after mistaking the camera's flash for firecrackers that villagers use to drive the herd from crops. And monkeys have been known to pose in front of the camera, running off whole rolls of film.

3 POOPER SCOOP SCIENCE

Moja, a black Labrador, ran through the forest brush. His nose was fixed on a favorite scent—scat—the droppings of a lynx. When he finds it, scientists will use this waste material to unlock the mysteries of these secretive cats.

The scat of an animal contains, among other things, cells from the lining of the animal's intestine. These cells, like all cells, contain its genetic material called DNA. And DNA is being used to answer many questions about endangered species. For example, it can determine the health of a population, identify individual animals, and map their family connections.

Dr. Sam Wasser, scientific director of the Center of Wildlife Conservation in Seattle, Washington, works in the field of genetics, the science that studies heredity, genes, and DNA. He pioneered a process of extracting DNA from scat and using it to aid conservation of endangered species. But he needed an efficient way to collect it. "I'm always thinking about how you can get more poop out of the woods," Wasser said. "Then it hit me: dogs."

DNA

Inside every living cell is the blueprint of life—genetic material called DNA (deoxyribonucleic acid). DNA contains instructions for how an organism is made. It controls the color of a tiger's stripes, the size of a lion's mane, and the shape of a cheetah's legs. DNA is coiled up in the center of the cell in threadlike strands called chromosomes. Sections of the chromosomes are called genes. Although most of the genes are the same for every animal in a species, other parts of DNA strands vary. These are the genes that scientists use to identify individual animals.

Dogs like Moja are trained in the same way police dogs are trained to sniff out narcotics. They can scent scat from 13 different species at the same time, locate scents from a half mile away, and up to 12 feet (3.6 meters) beneath the snow. These trained dogs allow researchers to collect enormous amounts of data and cover much more terrain than a person could alone.

Sam Wasser with Moja. Moja's keen sense of smell helps keep track of the elusive lynx population.

Snow Leopard (*Panthera uncia*)

The snow leopard lives in some of the most remote and snowy mountains of Central Asia. It has developed a thick, long fur coat with an extra long tail that can be wrapped around its face like a muffler. Its coat is smoky gray with dark gray rosettes, which gives it perfect camouflage in its snow-covered habitat. The snow leopard is much smaller than other big cats, growing only 4 feet (1.2 meters) in length with a 3-foot (0.9-meter)-long tail, and weighing from 80 to 165 pounds (36 to 75 kilograms). Their inhospitable habitat makes them one of the least-known cats, but researchers estimate that there are 4,000 to 6,000 remaining in the wild.

But the real wonder of this research is what Wasser and other genetic scientists can "read" from the scat. Using a process called PCR (polymerase chain reaction), Wasser is able to locate and read tiny fragments of DNA in scat. Certain sections of DNA show a lot of variation and can be used to identify an individual. In this way Wasser can accurately estimate how many animals are in a given area.

Before DNA tracking, a biologist would have to trap animals and mark them to determine the size of a population. But as Wasser explained, such sampling is not that accurate. Female animals for example are trap shy, which means they would not be figured in the count.

Lynx (*Lynx lynx*)

Although not a big cat, the lynx is another important carnivore in the United States. There are three subspecies of lynx, the Canadian, Eurasian, and Iberian (or Spanish). The Canadian lynx is rare in the northern United States, and is adapted to snowy mountain forests. These solitary cats are very similar to bobcats. They have long legs, short bodies, and a stubby tail. Their face is surrounded by a furry fringe and their ears end in pointed tufts. An adult male may weigh up to 23 pounds (10 kilograms). They hunt mainly rabbits.

Scat is especially useful when studying animals that are difficult to observe. Researchers in Nepal and Mongolia studying the snow leopard rarely see their elusive study animal, but they do see its scat, and it's much easier to scoop up the poop than track such a secretive cat.

Collecting scat is also noninvasive. That's important when dealing with a rare, endangered species or studying the stressful effects of environmental change. The level of certain hormones is a measure of stress in an animal's system. A hormone is a chemical an animal produces that regulates growth and other functions of the body. Measuring stress by trapping the cat and drawing blood would only add to the animal's stress. It wouldn't give an accurate picture of how the cat was handling changes in its environment, such as logging or spreading suburban communities.

Scat studies are used not only to monitor the lynx in Yellowstone National Park and snow leopards in Asia, but also for other animals including northern spotted owls, bald eagles, western black bears, black rhinos, and African elephants.

4. VETS ON THE WILD SIDE

It's not easy to give a 200-pound (91-kilogram) cat a physical, let alone doing it in a swamp while time ticks away until the animal wakes up. But that's one of the many jobs of a wildlife veterinarian. Some wildlife vets work in zoos, some work side by side with biologists in the field, and many do both. Vets may bring all their knowledge and training to the forests of Siberia, or the plains of Africa, where long waving grass replaces the shiny metal exam table, and a tree with a sling stands in for a large and accurate scale.

Vets work one animal at a time, but in the wild they also monitor the overall health of an entire population so that they can stop a wildlife health crisis before it starts. Knowing how healthy a population is can indicate how well the animals are handling the stresses of habitat loss and other environmental pressures. It lets wildlife managers know if their conservation efforts are helping.

LIFE LION

As habitats become smaller, animals are forced to live closer together, coming in contact with species of animals they had not been near before. Sometimes these close encounters have disastrous results.

In 1994 the chief veterinary officer of the Tanzania National Park in Africa, Melody Roelke, came face-to-face with a sick lion. It was flailing, jerking, and couldn't stand up. The lion died later that night. Seven more lions died over the next few weeks, and within a month one third of the lion population was sick.

Roelke performed autopsies on the dead lions and took blood samples from the survivors. Lab tests revealed that the lions had canine distemper, a disease spread by a virus that usually attacks dogs, hyenas, and jackals. Habitat changes and human encroachment had placed domestic animals in more frequent contact with

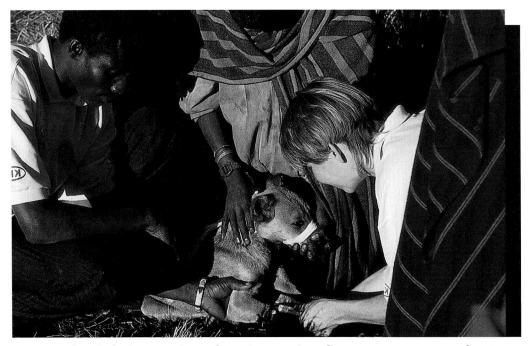

A dog is being vaccinated against canine distemper to prevent the spread of the disease.

wild animals allowing the disease to "jump species." Scientists believe that it spread from domestic dogs that lived near the park to hyenas that visited village garbage dumps and then to lions out in the wild.

To stop the disease from spreading further, scientists and vets started Project Life Lion, a vaccination program for dogs. Every year vets visit all the villages around the Tanzania National Park and vaccinate hundreds of dogs against canine distemper. So far it has kept this lion killer under control.

A FIELD CHECKUP

Field vets often accompany biologists who are capturing cats to be fitted with radio collars. It is their job to administer anesthetic, and check for signs of illness or injury. Simple things, such as a scratch or rash, can be cared for on site, but seriously ill cats may have to be taken to a zoo for further treatment.

During a panther's physical, the cat is weighed in a sling attached to a scale hanging from a nearby tree. It is given a vaccination for rabies and feline leukemia, and several vials of blood are drawn that will be used in lab tests and kept on file for future research. All this information is recorded and becomes part of the cat's medical history that will help biologists understand how the cat lives, and when it dies, the cause of death.

CATCH A TIGER BY THE TOE

One of Kathy Quigley's jobs as the wildlife veterinarian with the Hornocker Wildlife Institute at the University of Idaho in Moscow, Idaho is to train biologists in the use of tranquilizers so that they can safely give the drugs to big cats. She also cares for and examines Siberian tigers that have been captured for a radio collar for the Siberian Tiger Project. This partnership of wildlife researchers and vets is an important one. Each brings a different perspective to the project. Quigley knows cats, and wildlife researchers know population management.

Kathy Quigley checks the heart rate of an anesthetized Siberian tiger, Olga. She was the first wild Siberian tiger ever to be radio-collared and released. Olga has since grown and raised three litters of cubs.

"It takes months to find a tiger," Quigley explained. They look for a tiger's kills, check for scent trees that outline a tiger's territory, and set up spring-activated foot snares that trap a tiger uninjured. Each morning the scientists walk the trapline. "If a tiger is caught in a snare it usually just sits down and waits for us to come," she said.

Working with a tiger is a big change from vaccinating a pet. Although Quigley doesn't like to work on large cows and horses (they can kick you), she loves tigers. "Tigers are asleep when you work on them," she said. In less than an hour the research team can gather blood for DNA fingerprinting and lab tests, check the animal's health, and fit it with a radio collar. Then they start the search again for the next tiger.

TO THE RESCUE

The largest reserve in Central America, the Maya Biosphere Reserve, stretches over 6,000 square miles (15,540 square kilometers) and is home to the endangered jaguar. Although hundreds of jaguars may be poached each year, some of them are rescued by conservation officers and given a second chance in the wild.

But before a wild animal can be released, vets like Dr. Oscar Murga give it a checkup. Without a clean bill of health, there may be a risk of exposing other animals to a disease that the jaguar may be carrying. It could affect the whole ecosystem. The health of all wildlife plays an important role in keeping nature's web in balance. Jaguars, and smaller cats such as ocelots and margays, have all been safely returned to the Maya Biosphere Reserve.

VET INVENTIONS

Vets are always inventing new ways of performing difficult medical procedures and techniques to safely care for and study animals out in the wild.

"We could send men to the moon, but we couldn't get a tiny piece of tissue from a wild animal without capturing it first," said

Alan Rabinowitz has just put a radio-collar on this sedated male jaguar in Cockscomb Basin, Belize, and is now taking measurements.

Wendy Weisman, the program coordinator of the Field Vet Program at the Wildlife Conservation Society (WCS) in New York. Capturing an animal puts it under a lot of stress, and there is always danger of complications from anesthetic. But vets didn't have another alternative until Dr. William B. Karesh from WCS developed a skin biopsy dart. A biopsy is a medical procedure that removes a small sample of tissue from a living animal so that the sample can be examined more closely for signs of disease.

Instead of shooting an anesthetic into the animal, Karesh shoots the biopsy dart. In the center of the dart is a small barb or hook. A tiny piece of tissue sticks to the barb and is pulled off when the dart falls away from the animal. After the animal has left (annoyed, but uninjured), Karesh can safely collect the dart and the tiny piece of tissue.

Jaguar (*Panthera onca*)

The jaguar weighs up to 300 pounds (136 kilograms) and is the largest cat in the Americas. A jaguar looks like a larger, stronger cousin of the leopard. Its yellowish-orange coat is marked with large rosettes with smaller spots in the center. An all-black coat is just a color variation, with black spots on a black background. A jaguar's range is limited to pockets of remote tropical jungle and grasslands near rivers, lakes, and swamps in Mexico and Central and South America. At one time jaguars lived as far north as Tennessee, but today sightings in the southern region of the United States are very rare. These solitary hunters stalk many different animals, including monkeys, capybaras, snakes, and iguanas.

5 FROZEN ZOOS AND COMPUTER DATING

Did you know there are two subspecies of lion? There is the African lion that everybody knows, and the rare Asian lion that once roamed from Turkey to India. Today scientists believe that only 300 Asian lions are left in the wild, and they can only be found in the Gir National Park in Gujarat, west-central India. So when the Chester Zoo in England bred their Asian lions and three cubs were born, they increased the number of Asian lions by 1 percent. It may not sound like a lot, but it was a major accomplishment, and a big improvement.

One way to save the big cats is to create more of them. Breeding in zoos is called captive breeding and seems simple—to mate unrelated males and females of a species. Done systematically, it can increase a species' numbers and maintain the genetic diversity within a species.

Genetic Diversity

An offspring's genes are inherited through its parents—one half of its genetic makeup from its mother and one half from its father. All the genes represented in a group of animals are called the gene pool, and scientists believe that a healthy population has a wide range of different genes. This is genetic diversity. When only a few individuals of a species are left, the size of the gene pool is smaller. New offspring may be more vulnerable to genetic disease. To produce the healthiest offspring possible, scientists breed within an animal species only animals that are as distantly related as possible.

COMPUTER DATING

In the serious business of saving species, not just any animals can be mated. Decisions on which cats are bred are made by a group of experts who specialize in a particular species, such as the Siberian tiger. These committees make up the Species Survival Plans (SSP), which track and monitor all of the captive animals in that species. "The object of the SSP is to maintain the same genetic diversity in captivity as there would be in the wild," said Chris Kieber, curator of mammals at the Buffalo Zoological Gardens. Keeping subspecies separate is important. Cats in the same species have adapted to different climates and habitats. For example, Siberian tigers have thick fur and large bodies to keep them warm in Russian snowy winters, whereas tigers from the island of Sumatra are smaller and perfectly adapted to a tropical habitat. "If there was ever a chance to reintroduce captive cats back in the wild it would make a difference," Kieber said. "However, right now there is not enough wild for big cats to go back to."

A member of the SSP committee keeps track of each animal in a detailed and complex studbook. "There is a school to learn how to keep the studbook," Kieber said. "It involves a lot of math." Besides the basic information about the animal, it also includes

Scientists have successfully bred clouded leopards by artificial insemination.

complex mathematical equations that represent how much of that cat's genetic makeup is represented in the entire population.

Every captive animal is also given a number and included in a sophisticated computer system called the International Species Information System (ISIS). ISIS keeps track of most of the zoo animals in the world so that a clouded leopard in Buffalo might be mated with a clouded leopard in Australia.

But sometimes cats in captivity do not breed well. They frequently refuse to mate, and even maim or kill each other in the process, as clouded leopards are known to do. Wildlife scientists working in the fields of genetics and reproductive science are taking veterinary procedures originally developed for breeding domesticated animals and adapting them to wild cats and other animals.

TEST-TUBE KITTENS

Dr. David Wildt, a reproductive physiologist, and his colleagues at the Smithsonian's National Zoological Park in Washington, D.C., have been studying ways to increase the reproduction of big cats for many years. They can't afford to experiment with rare cheetahs or tigers because their populations are too small, but house cats are good models for their rarer cat cousins, and so scientists use domestic cats to research safe methods of cat reproduction.

One process called in vitro fertilization involves taking an egg from the female and fertilizing it in a test tube. The fertilized egg is then placed back in the mother where it will develop. This technique has been helping human parents for decades. If it worked for big cats it would mean that dangerous dates between an aggressive male and a picky female could be avoided.

In 1987, after two years of research, Dr. Wildt announced the birth of the first test-tube kittens. Since then several big cats have been born, including two tiger cubs. Another procedure called artificial insemination has produced clouded leopard and cheetah cubs, and female lions are playing surrogate, or substitute, mother to baby tigers and ocelots.

FROZEN ZOOS

Thousands of animals are housed in two small rooms at the Center for Reproduction of Endangered Species (CRES) at the San Diego Zoo. Tigers are kept next to the condors, and giraffes near gorillas. They don't eat or drink, they are kept safe from disease, and each takes up no more room than a plastic drinking straw. It is a cryogenic storage system called the frozen zoo.

The four futuristic freezers look like a set of washing machines, but are actually cryogenic (cold-generating) storage tanks. The material they hold is so precious that the second pair of freezers, holding similar material as the first pair, had to be moved to a separate building in case of a fire, power failure, or earthquake.

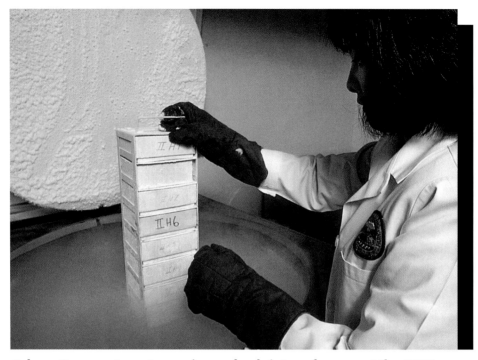

Arlene Kumamoto puts specimens back into a freezer at the CRES frozen zoo at the San Diego Zoo.

Stored inside the tanks is the genetic material of more than 3,200 animals kept at a chilling -385°F (-232°C). Liquid nitrogen, which mists up when the freezers are opened, is so cold that it can preserve living tissue for many years. It is a frozen insurance policy for the future, an almost endless supply of genetic diversity. Dr. Wildt believes that the ability to freeze genetic material is vital for endangered species because it can be used to increase the gene pool in later generations. The genetic material of animals long dead can be thawed and used to develop new offspring.

Originally the cell cultures were collected from animals at the San Diego Zoo during regular veterinary visits—taken from skin biopsies, from ear-notch samples, or from animals that had died. But now material comes from other zoos around the world and from researchers in the field. New ways of transporting the tissue in liquid nitrogen dry shippers allow biologists to take samples and freeze them in remote places before sending them to San Diego.

The CRES frozen zoo was started in 1975 by Dr. Kurt Benirschke, a medical doctor who began using his training on endangered animals. He saw a need to preserve genetic material for scientists to study genetic diseases, reproduction, and for taking DNA fingerprints.

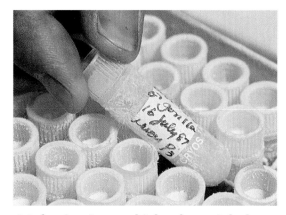

It's fascinating to think what might be created from genetic material stored at CRES.

But in 1997, when the first sheep named Dolly was cloned, the idea of creating an endangered animal in a laboratory became a real, yet still remote, possibility. Although the opportunity to clone endangered animals exists, scientists think it is too expensive and difficult, and too far in the future to be a useful conservation tool. Some scientists fear that such

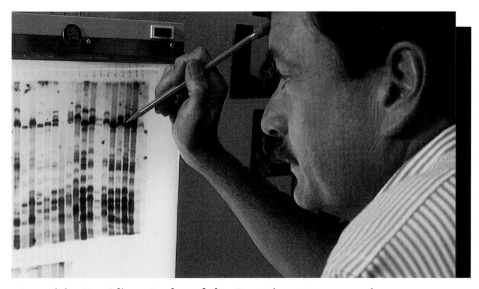

Geneticist Dr. Oliver Ryder of the San Diego Zoo examines electrotherograms of DNA fragments

Lion (*Panthera leo*)

Both the African lion and Asian lion are the most social of the big cats. They live in groups called prides, consisting of several females, their cubs, and a dominant male. They prey on wildebeests, zebras, impalas, and other large animals. The African and Asian lions weigh between 300 and 500 pounds (136 and 227 kilograms) and differ only slightly in appearance. Asian lions have a fold of skin along their abdomen, and a somewhat sparser mane on the males. The African lion lives throughout much of wild Africa, while the Asian lion lives only in the Gir National Park in India.

high-tech research might take away from the real issue of preserving habitats, saying that it would be meaningless to create animals when no habitat was available for them to live in.

Other scientists assert that the best argument for habitat preservation is preventing the extinction of a species using all the creative strategies that are available. Perhaps cloning may give conservationists a safety net for the future.

6 CHEETAH CHIRPS

Researcher Rachel Golden is eavesdropping on cheetah chat. With earphones on her head and holding a microphone, Golden listens while Shaba and Chafa, two six-year-old cheetah brothers at the National Zoological Park, call to each other with high-pitched chirping sounds. Listening to cheetah chat is just one way that scientists can better understand how these cats live in the wild and in captivity.

HAPPY CATS

Zoos are hard at work creating comfortable places for cats to live, but it's a difficult job when a wild cat's home range may be hundreds of miles and the zoo's space is limited to only hundreds of feet. Captive cats are kept healthy and safe, but some scientists wonder if that is enough.

Are cats in zoos the same as cats born in the wild? What makes a cheetah a cheetah? Is it just its spotted

Cheetah on the savanna in Masai Mara Reserve, Kenya

coat, lean legs, and cleatlike claws, or is it more? A wild cheetah behaves differently from any other cat and it is important to understand and preserve its behaviors in order to preserve the species.

The scientific study of an animal's behavior is called ethology, and ethologists, or behaviorists, are working in zoos across the country watching what makes cats such as the cheetah tick.

CHEETAH CHIRPS

Cheetahs do not breed easily in captivity, and scientists are not really sure why. At one time scientists thought it was because cheetahs are genetically similar to each other. Thousands of years ago, almost all of the wild cheetahs died off. The remaining small population that was left had little genetic diversity. Scientists call this a genetic bottleneck, a problem that can sometimes cause disease and birth defects. But recent behavioral studies suggest that cheetahs don't do well in captivity because of the way they are housed.

In the wild, lions and hyenas often steal a cheetah's food and prey on cheetah cubs. But in zoos, cheetahs are often housed in the same area, often within sight and sound of their worst enemy.

Cheetahs are different socially from every other cat. Wild male cheetahs form lifelong partnerships called coalitions with two to four other males, while females live solitary lives. The study at the National Zoological Park tested these relationships by listening to cheetahs call to each other when together and then separated. The results showed that the bonds between captive male cheetahs appear to be as strong as those in the wild. When cheetah males are housed together they rarely call to each other. But when separated for a ten-minute period some of the males made over 100 calls. They were probably trying to locate their coalition partner.

Someday, if the animals are to be released to the wild, the formation of these coalitions will be important, because wild males in a coalition survive longer, and have fewer diseases than males that go it alone.

Behaviorists at CRES studied the way female cheetahs use scent to communicate with males. Traditionally females and males were housed together. But new scent research showed that the cats bred better when housed separately. Every day the male is allowed to sniff the scents in the female's cage when she is not present. The male cheetah can pick up clues about the female's readiness to mate. Since the zoo managers learned to "read" the scent clues and have changed the cheetah's housing arrangements, several cheetah cubs have been born.

BORN TO HUNT?

Do animals born in captivity know the same things that animals born in the wild know? Do they know how to get food on their own, or how to hide from predators?

In 1977, Laurie Marker, currently director of the Cheetah Conservation Fund, set out to test the hunting skills of Khayam, a captive-born cheetah. She took Khayam to Namibia in Africa where wild cheetahs live. Khayam's first hunting trip proved to Marker

Laurie Marker with Chewbakka, the Cheetah Conservation Fund "ambassador" of education in Namibia

that he did not know how to hunt. After Marker spent two months teaching him how to stalk prey, Khayam finally caught a steenbok, a kind of antelope. But he did not know what to do with it. Marker had to clamp the cheetah's jaws down on the animal's neck to kill it.

As wild habitats continue to disappear it seems that for some animals the best conservation strategy is keeping them in captivity until the world is fully committed to saving their habitat. By understanding how wild cats act and helping them to stay "wild," the experts have a better chance of raising cats that someday may be able to be released back into their natural habitat.

FISH AND CINNAMON

Understanding a cat's behavior is one part of a zoo curator's problem, the other is giving cats the opportunity to act like cats. In the past big cats spent their time sleeping on the concrete floor, or pacing endlessly in front of the bars, but at zoos such as the Buffalo Zoological Garden and Metro Washington Park Zoo, big cats hunt for fish and search for pieces of meat that the keepers have hidden in logs. This allows the animals to forage and hunt for food as they would in the wild.

Dr. David Shepherdson coordinates the Metro Washington Park Zoo's captive enrichment program and is a pioneer in this new field of study. "An animal in the wild basically does only a few things. It hunts, eats, sleeps, often plays, and breeds. But when they don't have to hunt for food or engage in normal activities like playing or exploring, they can quickly become bored."

At the Buffalo Zoo it is keeper David Brigham's job to think up ways for captive cats to flex their muscles, and act like cats. He hides food and gives them large, tough boomer balls that the cats can bang around and pounce on as if they were prey. Captive enrichment is not a hard science, however. It's more of a guessing game as to what activities will keep a cat's attention and keep its instincts strong. "It's tough to think up new things," Brigham said. He has to use his imagination. Sometimes the thrill of a new toy or activity only lasts a few minutes.

It can be as simple as giving them a different smell. Brigham sprays perfume on hay or on a burlap bag and lets the cats rub and roll around on it. "The snow leopards like the smell of cinnamon," he said. They also put old branches, or even feces from another animal's cage into the enclosure for the cats to sniff.

Some ideas are more complicated. One time the keepers made a papier-mâché zebra, put food inside it, and placed it in the lions' enclosure facing the cats' entrance. At first the lions were cautious. They stalked it, attacking it from behind as they would in the wild.

Although some small Asian fishing cats enjoy live fish swimming in their pool, other cats are frightened by the new experience. Tigers love the water, so Shepherdson thought he'd put trout in one female tiger's pond. She didn't notice the fish until the keeper slowly started to lower the water level. When only 6 inches (15 cen-

Cheetah (*Acinonyx jubatus*)

Cheetahs are very different from other big cats. They are built for speed with a small head, large, long legs, and nonretractable claws that act like cleats digging into the soil. Weighing between 80 and 150 pounds (36 and 68 kilograms), they hunt gazelles, impalas, and other animals. There are two subspecies of cheetah, the rare King cheetah (above) that lives mainly in Iran, and the African cheetah, which thrives in open grasslands in sub-Saharan African countries such as Namibia, Botswana, and Zimbabwe. It is estimated that there are 12,500 cheetahs left in the wild.

timeters) of water was left, she finally saw the trout swimming toward her. "She was terrified," Shepherdson said.

Cheetahs are known for their incredible bursts of speed, but rarely get a chance to run in captivity. In order to give them some exercise some zoos use "lure coursing," originally used to run greyhounds. A zigzagging course is built with a half mile (.8 kilometer) of fishing line looped around pulleys that have been staked into the ground and attached to a motor. The National Zoological Park uses a plastic "strip" lure, but others simply use a plastic bag that is pulled through the course on the fishing line and coaxes the cheetahs to run up to 35 miles (56 kilometers) an hour.

Chasing a plastic bag around may not make a cheetah ready for the dangerous wilds of Africa, but it will preserve instincts that may otherwise disappear.

7   WILDLIFE DETECTIVES

A wildlife crime has been committed. There is a suspect and a crime scene, but the only thing left of the victim is a hair stuck to a knife. The chance of convicting the criminal with this kind of evidence is slim, unless a wildlife forensic scientist like Bonnie Yates is called in on the case.

Yates is a morphologist, a scientist who studies the physical differences between animal species. She works at the only full-service wildlife crime lab in the world, the National Fish and Wildlife Forensics Laboratory in Ashland, Oregon, where she helps solve crimes against nature. "Forensic" means that Yates's work can be used in a court of law, and the lab's main goal is to identify the species of the victim, determine cause of death, and link the suspect to both the victim and the crime scene.

Unfortunately poaching, and buying and selling animal products made from endangered species is a billion-dollar business. It's almost as big as the illegal trade in drugs. To slow the trade and prevent rare animals from

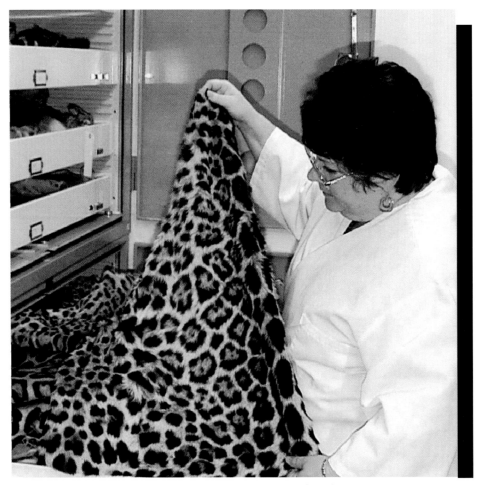

Bonnie Yates using the library at the National Fish and Wildlife Laboratory

becoming extinct, a treaty called the Convention on International Trade in Endangered Species (CITES) was written in the early 1970s and signed by more than 140 countries. But there are still many poachers selling their kills to dealers who make souvenirs, clothing, jewelry, and medicine. Fortunately, there are also wildlife agents trying to catch these criminals.

But in order to convict the poachers, the products have to be identified as being made from an endangered species. More than

200 federal fish and wildlife agents, 80 wildlife inspectors at U.S. ports of entry, as well as state and international agencies send evidence to the lab for analysis. Before the forensic lab opened in 1989 it was difficult for wildlife conservation officers to get a conviction, but with the help of Bonnie Yates and other scientists more cases are being made.

Yates's job is to identify the evidence (which is also the victim). Her tools are her eyes, a microscope, and a museum-size collection of dead bodies. All kinds of animals come through her lab, but Yates estimates that about 20 percent of her cases involve endangered big cats. A whole tiger is easy to identify, but at the lab, Yates may only receive products made from cats, such as a leopard coat, jaguar shoes, a tiger-claw necklace, a small stuffed leopard cat sold in Asia as a souvenir, a pelt, a box of bones, or a single hair. And she usually has no idea where the evidence has come from.

It is difficult, but rewarding work. "I love what I do," Yates said. The evidence is sometimes gruesome and means that a rare wild animal was cruelly killed. But in the back of her mind Yates knows that her work may stop a poacher. All the scientists at the lab are helping to build this new science of wildlife forensics, and with each new case they experiment and find new ways to analyze the evidence. Ken Goddard, director of the lab admits, "It's a fun area. It's nice to explore a new field of science, and solve crimes too."

A HAIR OF A CHANCE

A common piece of evidence that Bonnie Yates examines may be just a piece of fur or hair. Working at her lab table she examines the fur first to assess where on the animal's body it came from. There are many different kinds of hair—whiskers, under fur, and several types of guard hairs—all on one animal. "I can tell belly fur from back fur," she said. "And I know what characteristics to look for."

A large patch of fur is easier to identify because she can also examine patterns in the fur. For example, she knows that a jaguar pelt differs from a leopard's because the jaguar pattern has smaller

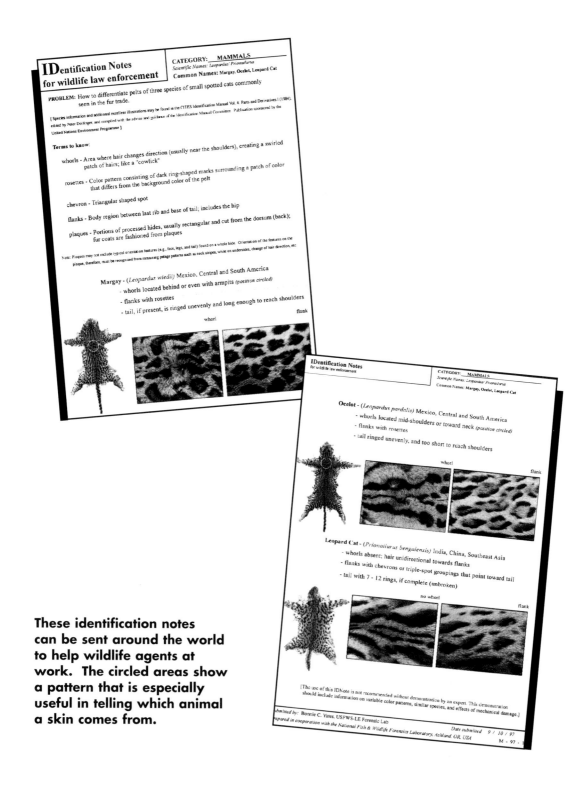

IDentification Notes
for wildlife law enforcement

CATEGORY: __MAMMALS__
Scientific Names: Leopardus/ Prionailurus
Common Names: Margay, Ocelot, Leopard Cat

PROBLEM: How to differentiate pelts of three species of small spotted cats commonly seen in the fur trade.

[Species information and additional excellent illustrations may be found in the CITES Identification Manual Vol. 4: Parts and Derivatives I (1984), edited by Peter Dollinger, and compiled with the advice and guidance of the Identification Manual Committee. Publication sponsored by the United Nations Environment Programme]

Terms to know:

whorls - Area where hair changes direction (usually near the shoulders), creating a swirled patch of hairs; like a "cowlick"

rosettes - Color pattern consisting of dark ring-shaped marks surrounding a patch of color that differs from the background color of the pelt

chevron - Triangular shaped spot

flanks - Body region between last rib and base of tail; includes the hip

plaques - Portions of processed hides, usually rectangular and cut from the dorsum (back); fur coats are fashioned from plaques

Note: Plaques may not include typical orientation features (e.g., face, legs, and tail) found on a whole hide. Orientation of the features on the plaque, therefore, must be recognized from remaining pelage patterns such as neck stripes, white on undersides, change of hair direction, etc.

Margay - (*Leopardus wiedii*) Mexico, Central and South America
- whorls located behind or even with armpits *(position circled)*
- flanks with rosettes
- tail, if present, is ringed unevenly and long enough to reach shoulders

whorl   flank

IDentification Notes
for wildlife law enforcement

CATEGORY: __MAMMALS__
Scientific Names: Leopardus/ Prionailurus
Common Names: Margay, Ocelot, Leopard Cat

Ocelot - (*Leopardus pardalis*) Mexico, Central and South America
- whorls located mid-shoulders or toward neck *(position circled)*
- flanks with rosettes
- tail ringed unevenly, and too short to reach shoulders

whorl   flank

Leopard Cat - (*Prionailurus bengalensis*) India, China, Southeast Asia
- whorls absent; hair unidirectional towards flanks
- flanks with chevrons or triple-spot groupings that point toward tail
- tail with 7 - 12 rings, if complete (unbroken)

no whorl   flank

[The use of this IDNote is not recommended without demonstration by an expert. This demonstration should include information on variable color patterns, similar species, and effects of mechanical damage.]

Submitted by: Bonnie C. Yates, USFWS-LE Forensic Lab
Prepared in cooperation with the National Fish & Wildlife Forensics Laboratory, Ashland, OR, USA

Date submitted   9 / 10 / 97
M - 97 -

These identification notes can be sent around the world to help wildlife agents at work. The circled areas show a pattern that is especially useful in telling which animal a skin comes from.

spots inside of the large circles. A leopard's spots do not have the inner marks. Plain, one-colored cats such as the Golden cat of Asia are harder to identify.

But even a single hair can tell a story. Every type of hair has certain characteristics that Yates has learned to identify. "A hair is like a pencil," she said. "The middle of the hair, called the medulla, is like the lead of the pencil. The surrounding part of the hair, called the cortex, would be like the wood of a pencil, and the cuticle of a hair would be like the paint on a number two pencil. That's where you find characteristic scales." Yates said. "A wolf hair, for example, has a dark-colored medulla like a cat's, but the cat's medulla has finely serrated edges. So I look for all these features that I know point in one direction to a family of animals."

FINDING THE PERFECT MATCH

When analyzing hair or fur, Yates uses a large collection of animal furs called reference standards. This collection is much like a museum collection, with examples of all different kinds of animals. She has all the different sizes of hairs from the back, face, belly, and feet of an animal as well as all the color variations. So if she thinks she has a cougar hair, Yates can compare the evidence hair to the reference hair and (hopefully) make a match.

SKIN AND BONES

Sometimes Yates receives a set of bones to identify. One case she worked on involved a man who illegally brought a tiger's skin and bones into the United States. Investigators found a torn photograph in a motel wastebasket that showed the bones and skin laid out together. But when investigators caught up with the man, he had only the bones in his possession. To make the case, Yates had to prove that the bones the investigators recovered were the same bones pictured in the photograph. Fortunately, the tissue still left on the bones had dried in an unusual way. Yates enlarged the photo, compared the tissue patterns, made a match, and the case was closed.

TIGER POWER

Some experts estimate that as many as a thousand tigers are killed by poachers each year. Wildlife agents believe that one of the biggest reasons for the poaching is the use of traditional Asian medicines. For many centuries people have believed that medicine made from various parts of the tiger can cure all sorts of illnesses and make a person strong. In two years China reportedly exported more than 27 million tiger-based products to 26 countries, including the United States.

But today there are fewer than 7,000 tigers left in the wild, and killing tigers for medicine takes a huge toll on their small population. "Anything to do with a tiger is very valuable," Yates said. "And as the tigers get more rare, other animals are being substituted for them." Wildlife agents suspect that even jaguars in South America and cougars in the United States are being killed and their bones sent to Asia.

THE MEDICINE TEST

Down the hall from Yates's morphology lab there is another group of scientists who analyze traditional Asian medicines to see if they contain tiger bone and other endangered species parts such as rhino horn. It's not an easy job. In order to make the medicines, the bone is usually burned and powdered until there are no identifying features left. "Tiger bones are tricky," Goddard said. "It's difficult enough if you have the whole bone, but we usually get preparations ground up. We may receive either tiger bone poultice that you'd put on an injury, tiger bone juice, or tiger bone wine." The potions are analyzed using various chemicals to find traces of calcium, which is the main ingredient in bone.

The good news is that calcium has been found in only a few of the medicines that the lab has analyzed so far. This means that most of the medicines are not illegal. The bad news is that this does not stop the poaching. Wildlife agents will have to keep looking for clues as to who is poaching and why. But it is certain that if tiger parts and other endangered species are being used illegally, the forensic scientists will be on the case.

Leopard (*Panthera pardus*)

Leopards live in bush and forest habitats throughout Africa, Asia, and the Far East. There are estimated to be as many as half a million leopards in sub-Saharan Africa, but in other parts of its range it is endangered. Weighing between 80 and 200 pounds (36 and 91 kilograms), the leopard is an agile climber and jumper, and preys on antelope, deer, wild pigs, and other animals. The clouded leopard (*Neofelis nebulosa*), the smallest of the big cats, weighs only 50 pounds (23 kilograms) and spends much of its time in trees.

8 ROOM TO ROAM

All over India, where villages meet the forest, tigers spend most of their day within hearing distance of human voices. Tigers require more space to survive than almost any other land animal, and in Russia, a male Siberian tiger may have a range as big as 500 to 620 square miles (1,295 to 1,605 square kilometers).

The tiger's main problem is space. The biggest threat to the territory of all big cats is the fragmentation, or chopping up, of large tracts of land. The Siberian tiger survives in only one tenth its former range, while the jaguar's habitat in Brazil has been cut at a rate of 5 million acres (2,025,000 hectares) a year. Logging is destroying whole forests, and the building of roads is opening up once remote places to poachers.

But now it's time to put some of the pieces of the habitat jigsaw puzzle back together again. Large carnivores won't survive unless we share the land with them. Scientists who study the interaction between animals and their habitat are called ecologists, and they are working together with other researchers to develop better ways for people and cats to live together.

BUILDING BLOCKS AND COMPUTER CONSERVATION

Identifying good, cat-friendly habitats—ones with plenty of prey, plant cover, and available mates—is the first step to habitat conservation. In the past, land that was inhospitable to man was set aside for nature sanctuaries without a thought as to whether the area provided the right sort of environment for the animals that would live there.

Scientists at the World Wildlife Fund identified important tiger habitats with the help of high-tech computer models. They developed a system of Tiger Conservation Units (TCUs), which are blocks of habitat where tigers could survive. The scientists analyzed hundreds of maps to identify roads, railroads, cities, villages and farmland, and any other feature that could potentially restrict a tiger's movements. They put all of this data into a complex computer system called Geographic Information Systems (GIS). GIS was designed to take data from all sorts of sources, such as the field scientist, satellites, and road maps, and create maps of an animal's habitat.

GIS identified 159 TCUs. Each habitat unit was ranked by how tiger friendly it was. A good habitat was large, intact, had little poaching, and a healthy population of tigers. Once identified, these areas can be managed by government and conservation agencies. The Indian government, for example, has moved entire villages out of prime tiger habitat and closer to markets and towns. Plantations of mangroves have been planted along park edges so that people can use these trees for fuel instead of moving into the forests for wood.

SAFE PASSAGE

In spite of major conservation efforts, recent maps based on satellite data revealed that tiger habitats had become isolated patches. "You can't hide from the satellite," said John Seidensticker, curator

A View From the Stars

Satellite imagery, originally developed for the military, is now answering important questions about habitats and how they change. It gives scientists a global view of the world they couldn't get any other way.

A satellite is equipped with various sensors that take pictures of the earth's surface, and measure and record data at regular intervals. There are many different kinds of sensors that detect various wavelengths of light. Data from each sensor can differentiate between land and water, natural features or man-made materials, identify plant species, or determine healthy or diseased plants.

The satellite views the earth's surface in small square units called pixels, which contain information about a certain area of land. Connecting the pixels creates a satellite image of a larger area. If you look at a television screen through a magnifying glass you see small individual dots of color. Each dot is a pixel. Back away and the pixels blend into a recognizable picture.

The data is collected and converted into numbers, which are transmitted, stored, and displayed by computers. The digital data is used to create maps and images of the earth's surface for scientists to analyze. Images taken of the same area over many months or years will show changes in the earth's surface over time—changes made by man, such as logging or spreading communities, and natural changes, such as fires or flooding.

of mammals with the Smithsonian Institution and chairman of Save the Tiger Fund. "Its images show exactly what was happening to the tigers' habitat." It was clear that setting aside land was only one part of the solution. Left alone, these habitats become islands surrounded by man-made communities and farms.

Now scientists are trying to link the habitats with wildlife corridors, strips of land connecting two, much larger patches. Animals would no longer be isolated and could move from one territory to another in search of food and mates. Wildlife corridors have been used in Australia, and they also help jaguars move freely in and out of rainforest reserves in Costa Rica.

ALLIGATOR ALLEY—
DESIGNING A SAFER HIGHWAY

There is a road in Florida called "alligator alley." It runs across the state from the Gulf of Mexico to the Atlantic coast. But it also runs through prime panther country. From 1979 to 1989, 12 panthers were killed on southwest Florida roads, 5 of them on alligator alley. With the panther population tipping the scale at 50, each death was a tragedy. Talk about widening the road to improve safety for people caused further concern from panther supporters. The cats would have to run farther and faster to get across the wider road safely.

Gary Evink, chief ecologist for the Department of Transportation, and Tom Logan, then bureau chief of wildlife for the Florida Game and Fresh Water Fish Commission, teamed up to design panther-safe underpasses. To decide where to put the underpasses, Logan and Evink relied on the data gathered from the radio-tracked cats. Records of panther accidents and computer models

Panther underpasses at Alligator Alley, Florida, were built especially to save the remaining Florida panthers.

The underpasses work! A Florida panther triggers a remote camera at an Alligator Alley underpass.

pinpointed places where collared panthers crossed the road most often. Thirty-six underpasses were created, each 8 feet (2.4 meters) tall and 100 feet (30.5 meters) wide. Sections of tall fencing were built on either side of the road so that animals were encouraged to cross only at the underpasses. To prove that it worked, a remote-sensing camera was set up. The first roll of film showed a radio-collared panther, four deer, and a man on a motorcycle. Since then the underpasses engineered to help panthers have also helped bobcats, raccoons, opossums, and alligators.

PEOPLE POWER

Saving the big cats of the world must involve the people who live close to them. Sometimes that means making safer highways or setting aside large tracts of land for wildlife. And in other parts of the world, scientists and government officials are working closely with communities to make sure that the people who gain the most from killing tigers, snow leopards, or cougars also gain the most by protecting them.

Conserving such predators is a tough sell. The snow leopard's skin is worth more than 60 times what a person might earn in a year in the country of Kyrgyzstan. Two pounds (1 kilogram) of tiger bone, ground down to make medicine can be sold for $2,000. These carnivores are also killed as pests because they are a deadly nuisance to farmers' livestock.

But one organization, called the International Snow Leopard Trust, has been successful in involving people in conservation, and making them partners with scientists. In Pakistan, human hunters and snow leopards compete for the snow leopard's favorite prey, the wild ibex. Fewer ibex mean that snow leopards will be more likely to attack and kill a farmer's cattle. An arrangement was made that will help the farmer as well as the leopard. Pakistani families agreed to stop hunting the wild ibex for three years. As a result the ibex population is increasing. In return for the hunting ban, conservationists have agreed to pay the local people salaries to act as game wardens to protect the area's wildlife.

In Nepal, conservationists hold town meetings so that villagers can share in making decisions for ways to protect the snow leopard as well as their livelihood. And in Mongolia, farmers are taught better ways to make leopard-proof fences.

People in the United States are making a difference too. Some volunteer at zoos to teach visitors about wild cats, and help raise orphaned cubs in zoo nurseries. Others help with wildlife studies, or support conservation groups that work in countries around the world. Even a class of fourth graders at Pierce Elementary School in Birmingham, Michigan, made a difference. They raised money for snow-leopard research.

People living near big-cat habitats are also becoming more aware of the amazing creatures that they share the land with. In 1982 the Florida panther was named the official Florida State animal.

But it takes more than honoring a wild animal to protect it. Researchers from all fields of science are sharing their knowledge with wildlife conservationists to make sure that wild cats survive. All of the high-tech equipment, extensive research, diligent observations, and painstaking planning will work, but only if people are willing to share the planet with the most beautiful and dangerous creatures on earth—the big cats.

GLOSSARY

biology—the study of living things

biopsy—a medical procedure to remove a tiny piece of tissue for study

cryogenics—a process of cold storage that preserves living tissue at extremely cold temperatures

DNA—deoxyribonucleic acid, the molecule in cells that contains coded genetic information

ecology—the study of the relationship between animals, people, and the environment

ethology—the scientific study of animal behavior

forensic science—a field of science that can be used in a court of law

genetics—the science of heredity and the way living things vary

habitat—the place where an animal lives in nature

morphology—the scientific study of the physical differences between animal species

physiology—the study of how a living thing works

scat—animal feces, or droppings

subspecies—a separation of a species based on geography or physical differences

wildlife corridor—a narrow band of wild land that connects two larger patches of land

FURTHER READING

For more information on big cats and how scientists work, check out these and other books.

Clark, Margaret Goff. *The Endangered Florida Panther.* New York: Cobblehill Books, 1993. Discusses the plight of the panther and what biologists are doing to protect the species.

Irvine, Georgeanne. *Blanca and Arusha: Tales of Two Big Cats.* New York: Simon & Schuster, 1995. Tells the story of a captive cheetah and a white tiger at the San Diego Zoo. It also includes facts about big cats.

Sayre, April Pulley. *Put on Some Antlers and Walk Like a Moose.* New York: Twenty-First Century Books, 1997. Talks about how scientists track all kinds of wild animals.

Seidensticker, John. *Tigers.* Minnesota: Voyageur Press, 1996. A beautiful book about tigers and how they are being studied in India.

INTERNET INFORMATION

Sites on the Internet change quickly, however, here are a few sites where you can learn more about big cats and conservation:

International Snow Leopard Trust at http://www.serv.net/islt/

National Wildlife Federation at http://www.nwf.org/nwf

The Tiger Information Center at http://www.5tigers.org

The Wild Habitat at http://tqd.advanced.org/11234/index.html

Look up your favorite zoo on ZooNet.com

INDEX